POETRY FOR YOUNG PEOPLE

Langston Hughes

Edited by Arnold Rampersad & David Roessel
Illustrations by Benny Andrews

STERLING

New York / London
www.sterlingpublishing.com/kids

To Casey, Julien, Sahara and Jesse.
—B.A.

STERLING and the distinctive Sterling logo are registered trademarks of Sterling Publishing Co., Inc.

Library of Congress Cataloging-in-Publication Data

Hughes, Langston, 1902-1967.
Langston Hughes / edited by Arnold Rampersad & David Roessel ; illustrations by Benny Andrews.
p. cm. -- (Poetry for young people)
Includes index.
ISBN-13: 978-1-4027-1845-8
ISBN-10: 1-4027-1845-4
1. African Americans--Juvenile poetry. 2. Children's poetry, American. I. Rampersad, Arnold.
II. Roessel, David E. (David Ernest), 1954- III. Andrews, Benny, 1930- ill. IV. Title. V. Series.

PS3515.U274A6 2006
811'.52--dc22

2005025369

2 4 6 8 10 9 7 5 3 1

Published by Sterling Publishing Co., Inc.
387 Park Avenue South, New York, NY 10016
Published by arrangement with Alfred A. Knopf, a division of Random House, Inc.
© 1994 by the Estate of Langston Hughes
Editorial material © 2006 by Arnold Rampersad and David Roessel
Artwork © 2006 by Benny Andrews
Photograph of Langston Hughes on page 4 © Corbis
Distributed in Canada by Sterling Publishing
$^c/_o$ Canadian Manda Group, 165 Dufferin Street
Toronto, Ontario, Canada M6K 3H6
Distributed in the United Kingdom by GMC Distribution Services
Castle Place, 166 High Street, Lewes, East Sussex, England BN7 1XU
Distributed in Australia by Capricorn Link (Australia) Pty. Ltd.
P.O. Box 704, Windsor, NSW 2756, Australia

Printed in China
All rights reserved

Sterling ISBN-13: 978-1-4027-5884-3
ISBN-10: 1-4027-5884-7

CONTENTS

INTRODUCTION

From the 1920s until his death in 1967, Langston Hughes was probably the foremost poet among African Americans. His importance for later African-American literature has been immense, for he sought not only to "sing" of Black America in his poems, but also to do so in its everyday language. Hughes was one of the first and most successful writers to incorporate African-American musical traditions like jazz, blues, and spirituals, into literature.

He was born James Langston Hughes in Joplin, Missouri, on February 1, 1902. His parents were not well matched, and Hughes's father, a businessman, soon left to seek employment, first in Cuba and later in Mexico. For much of his childhood, Hughes lived with his maternal grandmother in Lawrence, Kansas, while his mother worked in various low-paying jobs even as she dreamed of being an actress. He was a lonely child, and he mainly had books and his grandmother's stories for entertainment. In his autobiography, *The Big Sea*, Hughes remembered how, as he sat in his grandmother's lap, "she told me long, beautiful stories about people who wanted to make the Negroes free." He immortalized these evenings with his grandmother in the poem "Aunt Sue's Stories."

Hughes learned different lessons from his parents, neither of whom encouraged his poetic aspirations. His mother wanted him to take a responsible job early in his adult life, rather than continue his education. Following his high school graduation, he spent a painful year with his father in Mexico, where they soon clashed on a major issue: "My father hated Negroes. I think he hated himself, too, for being a Negro." Several of Hughes's early poems explored the dignity and beauty of African-American identity. To some degree, poems such as "My People" are a response to his father's attitude.

Hughes first saw Harlem in 1921, when he went to New York City to enroll at Columbia University. Leaving Columbia after his freshman year, he worked, among other places, as a dining hall worker on a ship sailing to Africa, in the kitchen of a Paris nightclub, and at a number of equally humble jobs in Washington, D.C.

Just as Aunt Sue never got her stories out of any book, so Hughes would not find his poetic inspiration in a library. At the opening of *The Big Sea*, Hughes relates how, as a seaman on his first trip to Africa in 1923, he threw all of the books that he had with him into the sea. This was a dramatic way of signaling his break with books in favor of the oral and musical traditions of black culture. We have evidence, however, that he kept one book—his copy of Walt Whitman's *Leaves of Grass,* for he "had no intention of throwing that one away." To the end of his life Whitman's verse would remain his main example that poetry could and should be made out of the speech of ordinary Americans.

Hughes, then, sought his material in the world around him. "Seventh Street in Washington," he wrote, was "the long, old, dirty street where ordinary Negroes hang out. On Seventh Street they played the blues, ate watermelon, shot pool, told tall tales, and looked at the Dome of the Capitol and laughed out loud. I listened to their blues. And I went to their churches and heard the tambourines play and the little tinkling bells of the triangle adorn the gay shouting that sent sisters dancing down the aisle for joy. I tried to write poems like the songs they sang on South Street, . . . songs that had the pulse beat of the people who keep going. Like the waves of a sea coming one after another, so is the undertow of black music with its rhythm that never betrays you, its strength like the beat of a human heart, its humor, and its living power."

As a busboy in Washington, Hughes made up blues poems in his head and sung them on the way to work. Unfortunately, he could not carry a tune. "One evening," he relates, "I was singing a blues [tune] I was trying to get down before putting it on paper. A man passing on the other side of the bridge stopped, looked at me and asked, 'What's the matter, son? Are you ill?' 'No,' I said, 'just singing.' 'I thought you were groaning,' he answered."

Despite his moves and travels, Harlem remained central in his life during the 1920s. This was the period of the Harlem Renaissance, when a vibrant group of young African-American writers and artists transformed African-American culture. They included brilliant writers such as Countee Cullen, Zora Neale Hurston, and Sterling Brown. The African-American journals that published many of Hughes's poems were based there. He drew heavily upon the urban experience in his work.

In 1925, Hughes published "The Weary Blues," his first experiment in the incorporation of African-American musical motifs from the blues, jazz, and spirituals into his verse. This poem, which won first prize in a poetry contest sponsored by the African-American magazine *Opportunity*, was perhaps the first successful attempt to incorporate the blues into American poetry.

He also employed elements of spirituals from the African-American church in the final version of the poem "When Sue Wears Red." Adding references to trumpets in the 1924 version of the poem was an example of Hughes's conscious effort to employ African-American elements in his work—the first version of the poem lacked those wonderful fanfares. What seems so simple and natural in the later version was actually arrived at only after careful thought.

In 1926, with the help of a wealthy friend, Hughes enrolled at Lincoln University in Pennsylvania, from which he graduated in 1929. While there, as he continued writing, he expressed the philosophy of the Harlem Renaissance writers in a landmark essay entitled "The Negro Artist and the Racial Mountain." It ends: "We younger Negro artists who create now intend to express our individual dark-skinned selves without fear or shame. If white people are pleased we are glad. If they are not, it doesn't matter. We know we are beautiful. And ugly too. The tom-tom laughs and the tom-tom cries. If colored people are pleased we are glad. If they are not, their displeasure doesn't matter either. We build our temples for tomorrow, strong as we know how, and we stand on the top of the mountain, free within ourselves."

This statement, however, offended some members of the black community, including church ministers and many lay people devoted to middle-class values. The response to his second book of poems, published in 1927, in which musical motifs from jazz and the blues are pronounced, was quite hostile. Hughes commented: "The Negro critics and many of the intellectuals were very sensitive about their race in books. In anything that white people were likely to read, they wanted to put their best foot forward, their politely polished and cultural foot, and only that foot. There was a reason for it of course. They had seen their race laughed at and caricatured so often." Hughes tried to stick to his artistic principles but had to refrain from reading blues poems in churches where the ministers objected to them. He needed and wanted the financial and emotional support of the black community.

Although Hughes's poetry always showed his strong commitment to social justice, in the 1930s (during the Great Depression) his political beliefs turned radical. While never a member of the Communist Party and cautious with his public dealings with Communists, he published several poems in their various journals. In 1932 he traveled to Moscow to work on a film about race relations but the project was never completed. However, Moscow had impressed him as a city with no color barriers, and he stayed for a year in what was then the Soviet Union.

Hughes was interested in other forms of literature besides poetry. In the 1930s, he wrote more than nine plays. In 1935, his tragedy *Mulatto* became the first play by an African American to appear on Broadway. He also collaborated with Zora Neale Hurston on *Mule Bone*; however, the authors had a falling out before its opening and the play was not produced until 1991 in New York. Hughes also had an interest in children's books. His classic story *Popo and Fifina*, written with Arna Bontemps, came out in 1932. A collection of short stories, *The Ways of White Folks* (1934), comments on how, fifty years after the end of slavery, whites still look upon African Americans as servants or possessions.

In the 1940s, Hughes moved to Harlem and made it his home for the rest of his life. In his first book of poems published after the move, *Shakespeare in Harlem*, he returned to writing as a "folk poet," with many of his pieces dealing with the blues, race, and segregation. In poetry and prose, he became a major voice calling for equal treatment for African Americans in the armed forces after the U.S. entered World War II. To this end, Hughes created one of his most popular characters, Jesse B. Semple (called "Simple"), first for a column in the newspaper *The Chicago Defender* and later for several collections of short stories. Simple is a Harlem everyman who converses with a more educated companion in Paddy's Bar. At first, Simple talks mainly about the war and segregation, but soon branches out to discuss his relations with his wife (from whom he is separated), his girlfriend, and his landlady, among others. Simple's comments are filled with wordplay and puns that seem simple on the surface but often have deeper meanings.

One of Hughes's most remarkable and inventive poems is the book-length *Montage of a Dream Deferred*, published in 1951. Hughes wrote that "this poem on contemporary Harlem, like be-bop, is marked by conflicting changes, sudden nuances, sharp and impudent interjections, broken rhythms, and passages sometimes in the manner of a jam session." The poem is written in numerous separate parts that together present a forceful picture of Harlem within a framework like an epic poem's. Hughes's next volume of poetry, *Ask Your Mama: 12 Moods for Jazz* (1961), attempts to fuse words and music, providing musical notations and instructions for musical accompaniment. The basic theme is again the deferred dream of civil rights for all in America and the world at large. Hughes's last collection of poems, *The Panther and the Lash*, which came out shortly after his death in 1967, is dedicated to Rosa Parks, whose refusal to give up her seat on a bus sparked the Montgomery, Alabama bus boycott of 1955. This dedication signals Hughes's continuing concern with the civil rights movement at home and with the struggle to end colonialism abroad. While some of Hughes's poems show his impatience with the lack of progress toward the goal of genuine social and political equality, he never loses his belief in that goal.

For the most part, Hughes's black audience remained firmly loyal to him. On the whole, he reached a far wider audience than did most poets of his time. He appeared regularly in African-American newspapers and read his work repeatedly at churches and community centers. Some have suggested that much of Hughes's work is too "simple," because he wanted to reach this broad audience. However, he had too much respect for his people to want to talk down to them. For Hughes, the poet is not only a dreamer but also a dream keeper, with a powerful social and political dimension. Finally, Hughes's writing is more than a portrait of the life and culture of African Americans only. It is also a wonderful investigation into the racial, social, and political meanings of the American culture and language.

THE NEGRO SPEAKS OF RIVERS

Hughes described how he came to write this poem:"Now it was just sunset, and we crossed the Mississippi, slowly, over a long bridge. I looked out the window of the Pullman [train car] at the great muddy river flowing down toward the heart of the South, and I began to think what that river, the old Mississippi, had meant to Negroes in the past—how to be sold down the river was the worst fate that could overtake a slave in times of bondage.... Then I began to think about other rivers in our past...."

I've known rivers:
I've known rivers ancient as the world and older than the
      flow of human blood in human veins.

My soul has grown deep like the rivers.

I bathed in the Euphrates when dawns were young.
I built my hut near the Congo and it lulled me to sleep.
I looked upon the Nile and raised the pyramids above it.
I heard the singing of the Mississippi when Abe Lincoln
      went down to New Orleans, and I've seen its muddy
      bosom turn all golden in the sunset.

I've known rivers:
Ancient, dusky rivers.

My soul has grown deep like the rivers.

Euphrates—the longest river (2100 miles) in western Asia flowing from east central Turkey through Syria to Iraq
Congo—the longest river (2900 miles) in central Africa flowing from Zambia to the Atlantic Ocean
Nile—the world's longest river (4145 miles) flowing from Lake Victoria in central Africa to the Mediterranean Sea

Aunt Sue's Stories

Hughes recalled his maternal grandmother's stories:"Through my grandmother's stories life always moved, moved heroically toward an end. Nobody ever cried in my grandmother's stories. They worked, schemed or fought. But no crying."

Aunt Sue has a head full of stories.
Aunt Sue has a whole heart full of stories.
Summer nights on the front porch
Aunt Sue cuddles a brown-faced child to her bosom
And tells him stories.

Black slaves
Working in the hot sun,
And black slaves
Walking in the dewy night,
And black slaves
Singing sorrow songs on the banks of a mighty river
Mingle themselves softly
In the flow of old Aunt Sue's voice,
Mingle themselves softly
In the dark shadows that cross and recross
Aunt Sue's stories.

And the dark-faced child, listening,
Knows that Aunt Sue's stories are real stories,
He knows that Aunt Sue never got her stories
Out of any book at all,
But that they came
Right out of her own life.

The dark-faced child is quiet
Of a summer night
Listening to Aunt Sue's stories.

DANSE AFRICAINE

In this poem, Hughes captures the mood of native African dancing performed to a drumbeat. Hughes was one of the first American poets to incorporate African themes into his work.

The low beating of the tom-toms,
The slow beating of the tom-toms,
     Low ... slow
     Slow ... low—
     Stirs your blood.
        Dance!
A night-veiled girl
     Whirls softly into a
     Circle of light.
     Whirls softly... slowly,
Like a wisp of smoke around the fire—
     And the tom-toms beat,
     And the tom-toms beat,
And the low beating of the tom-toms
     Stirs your blood.

Tom-tom—*drum played with the hands or sticks*

MOTHER TO SON

Here a mother tells her son to continue to strive despite life's hardships.
The poem contains one of Hughes's most memorable lines: "Life for me
ain't been no crystal stair."

Well, son, I'll tell you:
Life for me ain't been no crystal stair.
It's had tacks in it,
And splinters,
And boards torn up,
And places with no carpet on the floor—
Bare.
But all the time
I'se been a-climbin' on,
And reachin' landin's,
And turnin' corners,
And sometimes goin' in the dark
Where there ain't been no light.
So boy, don't you turn back.
Don't you set down on the steps
'Cause you finds it's kinder hard.
Don't you fall now—
For I'se still goin', honey,
I'se still climbin',
And life for me ain't been no crystal stair.

I'se—dialect meaning either "I have" or "I am"

14

WHEN SUE WEARS RED

Hughes claimed that he wrote this poem for a girl he had met in high school:"I met her at a dance….She had big eyes and skin like rich chocolate. Sometimes she wore a red dress that was very becoming to her."

When Susanna Jones wears red
Her face is like an ancient cameo
Turned brown by the ages.

Come with a blast of   trumpets,
    Jesus!

When Susanna Jones wears red
A queen from some time-dead Egyptian night
Walks once again.

Blow trumpets, Jesus!

And the beauty of Susanna Jones in red
Burns in my heart a love-fire sharp like pain

Sweet silver trumpets,
    Jesus!

*Cameo—a gemstone carved in relief. The
    gemstone is usually a layered material
    with the relief in the top layer having a
    different color from the background.*

15

MY PEOPLE

Many of Hughes's best early poems explore the nature of, and the beauty in, the African element of African-American identity. This was one area where Hughes clashed with his father, and to some degree the poems were an answer to his father's negative attitude about Negroes.

The night is beautiful,
So the faces of my people.

The stars are beautiful,
So the eyes of my people.

Beautiful, also, is the sun.
Beautiful, also, are the souls of my people.

YOUTH

This early poem of Hughes conveys his
optimism, which he had not only for himself
but also for America.

We have tomorrow
Bright before us
Like a flame.

Yesterday
A night-gone thing,
A sun-down name.

And dawn-today
Broad arch above the road we came.

We march!

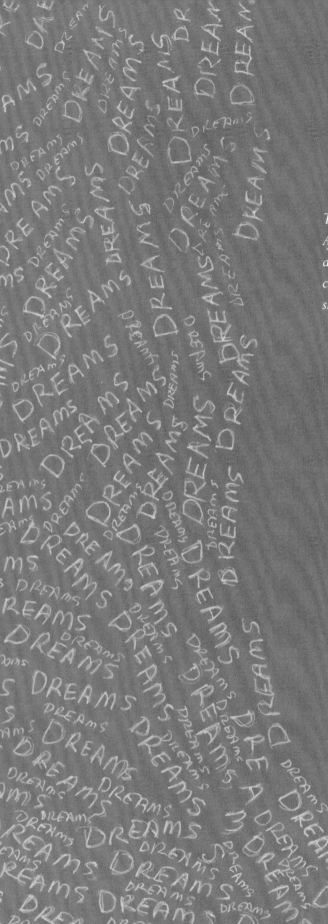

DREAM VARIATIONS

*This poem is another example of Hughes exploring the beauty of his
African-American identity. In a famous essay "The Negro Artist
and the Racial Mountain," he says: "We younger Negro artists who
create now intend to express our dark-skinned selves without fear or
shame....We know we are beautiful...."*

To fling my arms wide
In some place of the sun,
To whirl and to dance
Till the white day is done.
Then rest at cool evening
Beneath a tall tree
While night comes on gently,
    Dark like me—
That is my dream!

To fling my arms wide
In the face of the sun,
Dance! Whirl! Whirl!
Till the quick day is done.
Rest at pale evening . . .
A tall, slim tree . . .
Night coming tenderly
    Black like me.

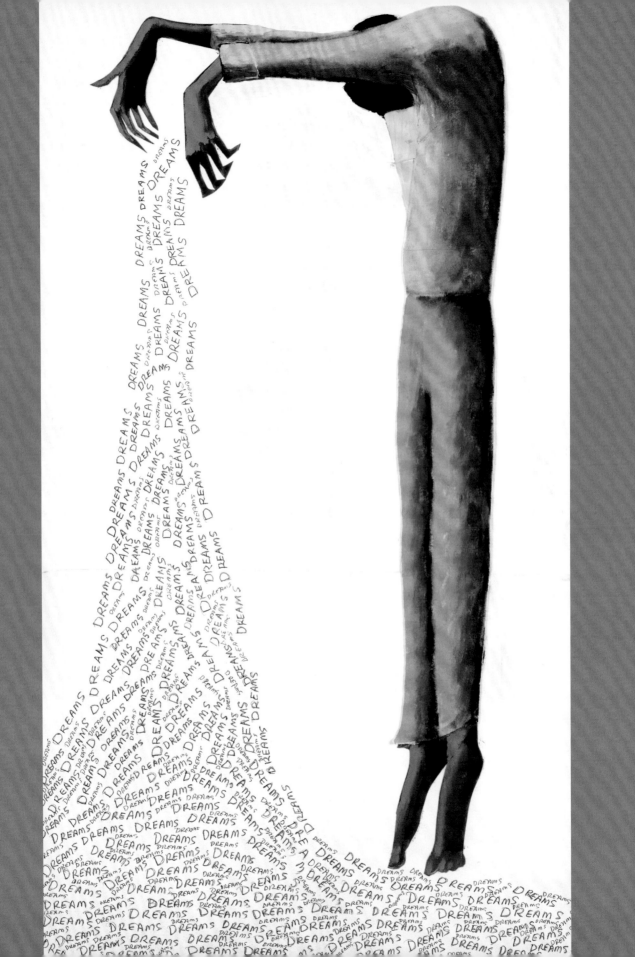

THE DREAM KEEPER

*Dreams are a recurring theme in Hughes's work. For Hughes,
poets are not just dreamers but dream keepers for their people.*

Bring me all of your dreams,
You dreamers,
Bring me all of your
Heart melodies
That I may wrap them
In a blue cloud-cloth
Away from the too-rough fingers
Of the world.

WALKERS WITH THE DAWN

Hughes uses the sun and the dawn to express his optimistic feelings. He uses a similar metaphor in the poem "Hey! Hey!"

Being walkers with the dawn and morning,
Walkers with the sun and morning,
We are not afraid of night,
Nor days of gloom,
Nor darkness—
Being walkers with the sun and morning.

I, Too

Hughes composed this poem in 1924 at the age of twenty-two, when he found himself broke in the Italian city of Genoa. The first line of this poem probably alludes to the poetry of Walt Whitman, the American poet who died ten years before Hughes was born. One of Whitman's poems is entitled "I Hear America Singing."

I, too, sing America.

I am the darker brother.
They send me to eat in the kitchen
When company comes,
But I laugh,
And eat well,
And grow strong.

Tomorrow,
I'll be at the table
When company comes.
Nobody'll dare
Say to me,
"Eat in the kitchen,"
Then.

Besides,
They'll see how beautiful I am
And be ashamed—

I, too, am America.

23

THE WEARY BLUES

Hughes called this "my lucky poem" after it won first prize in a literary contest sponsored by Opportunity *magazine in 1925. The poem includes the first blues verses he'd heard as a child growing up in Lawrence, Kansas. It is also one of the first poems where Hughes began to experiment with how to incorporate African-American musical motifs from the blues, jazz, and spirituals into his verse.*

Droning a drowsy syncopated tune,
Rocking back and forth to a mellow croon,
    I heard a Negro play.
Down on Lenox Avenue the other night
By the pale dull pallor of an old gas light
    He did a lazy sway. . . .
    He did a lazy sway. . . .
To the tune o' those Weary Blues.
With his ebony hands on each ivory key
He made that poor piano moan with melody.
    O Blues!
Swaying to and fro on his rickety stool
He played that sad raggy tune like a musical fool.
    Sweet Blues!
Coming from a black man's soul.
    O Blues!
In a deep song voice with a melancholy tone
I heard that Negro sing, that old piano moan—
    "Ain't got nobody in all this world,
      Ain't got nobody but ma self.
      I's gwine to quit ma frownin'
      And put ma troubles on the shelf."

Thump, thump, thump, went his foot on the floor.
He played a few chords then he sang some more—
    "I got the Weary Blues
      And I can't be satisfied.
      Got the Weary Blues
      And can't be satisfied—
      I ain't happy no mo'
      And I wish that I had died."
And far into the night he crooned that tune.
The stars went out and so did the moon.
The singer stopped playing and went to bed
While the Weary Blues echoed through his head.
He slept like a rock or a man that's dead.

Syncopated—a musical term meaning to have a shifted accent in a musical composition (for example, to begin on an unaccented beat and continue it through the next accented beat).

Croon—a gentle singing

Lenox Avenue—a boulevard (now called Malcolm X Boulevard) in the Harlem section of Manhattan in New York City. Lenox Avenue came to be associated with the spirit of Harlem.

HOMESICK BLUES

In this poem about homesickness, Hughes uses
a Southern dialect to emphasize the feeling.

De railroad bridge's
A sad song in de air.
De railroad bridge's
A sad song in de air.
Ever time de trains pass
I wants to go somewhere.

I went down to de station.
Ma heart was in ma mouth.
Went down to de station.
Heart was in ma mouth.
Lookin' for a box car
To roll me to de South.

Homesick blues, Lawd,
'S a terrible thing to have.
Homesick blues is
A terrible thing to have.
To keep from cryin'
I opens ma mouth an' laughs.

De—dialect for "the"
Ma—dialect for "my"

27

HEY!

This is a companion piece to the following poem, "Hey! Hey!", where both are constructed with the identical format but have opposite moods. Hughes uses a blues format where the first two lines are repeated.

Sun's a settin',
This is what I'm gonna sing.
Sun's a settin',
This is what I'm gonna sing:
I feels de blues a comin',
Wonder what de blues'll bring?

HEY! HEY!

*This is a companion piece to the previous
poem. While "Hey!" is more downbeat and
this poem more upbeat, Hughes ends with
the more optimistic piece.*

Sun's a risin',
This is gonna be ma song.
Sun's a risin',
This is gonna be ma song.
I could be blue but
I been blue all night long.

29

AFRO-AMERICAN FRAGMENT

Here Hughes talks about his yearning to better understand his African heritage.

So long,
So far away
Is Africa.
Not even memories alive
Save those that history books create,
Save those that songs
Beat back into the blood—
Beat out of blood with words sad-sung
In strange un-Negro tongue—
So long,
So far away
Is Africa.

Subdued and time-lost
Are the drums—and yet
Through some vast mist of race
There comes this song
I do not understand,
This song of atavistic land,
Of bitter yearnings lost
Without a place—
So long,
So far away
Is Africa's
Dark face.

GENIUS CHILD

This well-known poem has grim and powerful final lines that
indicate Hughes's personal despair at the time he wrote it.

This is a song for the genius child.
Sing it softly, for the song is wild.
Sing it softly as ever you can—
Lest the song get out of hand.

Nobody loves a genius child.

Can you love an eagle,
Tame or wild?

Wild or tame,
Can you love a monster
Of frightening name?

Nobody loves a genius child.

Kill him—and let his soul run wild!

NOTE ON COMMERCIAL THEATRE

Hughes comments on the use of blues music in theater and adaptations of comic opera. Although best known for his poetry, Hughes also wrote several plays for the theater including Mulatto *and the lyrics for* Black Nativity.

You've taken my blues and gone—
You sing 'em on Broadway
And you sing 'em in Hollywood Bowl,
And you mix 'em up with symphonies
And you fixed 'em
So they don't sound like me.
Yep, you done taken my blues and gone.

You also took my spirituals and gone.
You put me in *Macbeth* and *Carmen Jones*
And all kinds of *Swing Mikados*
And in everything but what's about me—
But someday somebody'll
Stand up and talk 'bout me,
And write about me—
Black and beautiful—
And sing about me,
And put on plays about me!
I reckon it'll be
Me myself!

Yes, it'll be me.

Broadway—*the name of the Manhattan street that gives its name to New York City's commercial theater district*
Hollywood Bowl—*amphitheater in Hollywood, California, used for musical performances. It is the home of the Los Angeles Philharmonic.*
Macbeth—play by William Shakespeare. A well known adaptation of Macbeth *set in Haiti was performed at the Lafayette Theatre in Harlem in 1930.*
Carmen Jones—a Broadway theater production adapted from Georges Bizet's comic opera, Carmen. *It premiered in 1943.*
Swing Mikados—an adaptation of the comic opera, The Mikado, *by W. S. Gilbert with the music of Sir Arthur Sullivan. The* Swing Mikado *was performed in New York in 1939.*

MERRY-GO-ROUND
COLORED CHILD AT CARNIVAL

Hughes wrote about several social and political issues. In an essay entitled "My Adventures as a Social Poet," Hughes said: "Try as I might to float off into the clouds, poverty and Jim Crow would grab me by the heels, and right back on earth I would land."

Where is the Jim Crow section
On this merry-go-round,
Mister, cause I want to ride?
Down South where I come from
White and colored
Can't sit side by side.
Down South on the train
There's a Jim Crow car.
On the bus we're put in the back—
But there ain't no back
To a merry-go-round!
Where's the horse
For a kid that's black?

Jim Crow—refers to the Jim Crow Laws that enforced segregation of blacks and whites and were adopted in the Southern states after the U.S. Civil War. These laws were overturned or repealed after World War II.

WORDS LIKE FREEDOM

Hughes's strong interest in his African heritage and American social and political injustices led him to express his feelings on freedom and liberty.

There are words like *Freedom*
Sweet and wonderful to say.
On my heartstrings freedom sings
All day everyday.

There are words like *Liberty*
That almost make me cry.
If you had known what I know
You would know why.

STILL HERE

Hughes often wrote poems about the African-American struggle for a better existence in a racially divided America. He never lost his belief that the struggle was worth it.

I been scared and battered.
My hopes the wind done scattered.
Snow has friz me, sun has baked me.
    Looks like between 'em
    They done tried to make me
Stop laughin', stop lovin', stop livin'—
    But I don't care!
    I'm still here!

Friz—*dialect for "froze"*

I DREAM A WORLD

Besides poetry, Hughes also was interested in drama and wrote several plays. This poem comes from his only opera, Troubled Island, *which he wrote with the composer William Grant Still.*

I dream a world where man
No other man will scorn,
Where love will bless the earth
And peace its paths adorn.
I dream a world where all
Will know sweet freedom's way,
Where greed no longer saps the soul
Nor avarice blights our day.
A world I dream where black or white,
Whatever race you be,
Will share the bounties of the earth
And every man is free,
Where wretchedness will hang its head
And joy, like a pearl,
Attends the needs of all mankind—
Of such I dream, my world!

FINAL CURVE

*In this short yet humorous poem, Hughes tells us that
if we can face our true self, then we can face anything.*

When you turn the corner
And you run into *yourself*
Then you know that you have turned
All the corners that are left.

THEME FOR ENGLISH B

The college described in this poem is City College of the City University of New York. Hughes did not attend this school but received a Bachelor of Arts degree from Lincoln University in Pennsylvania.

The instructor said,

> *Go home and write*
> *a page tonight.*
> *And let that page come out of you—*
> *Then, it will be true.*

I wonder if it's that simple?
I am twenty-two, colored, born in Winston-Salem.
I went to school there, then Durham, then here
to this college on the hill above Harlem.
I am the only colored student in my class.
The steps from the hill lead down into Harlem,
through a park, then I cross St. Nicholas,
Eighth Avenue, Seventh, and I come to the Y,
the Harlem Branch Y, where I take the elevator
up to my room, sit down, and write this page:

Winston-Salem and Durham—*cities in North Carolina*
Y—*shortened form of Young Men's Christian Association (YMCA)*

42

ENGLISH B

It's not easy to know what is true for you or me
at twenty-two, my age. But I guess I'm what
I feel and see and hear, Harlem, I hear you:
hear you, hear me—we two—you, me, talk on this page.
(I hear New York, too.) Me—who?
Well, I like to eat, sleep, drink, and be in love.
I like to work, read, learn, and understand life.
I like a pipe for a Christmas present,
or records—Bessie, bop, or Bach.
I guess being colored doesn't make me *not* like
the same things other folks like who are other races.
So will my page be colored that I write?
Being me, it will not be white.
But it will be
a part of you, instructor.
You are white—
yet a part of me, as I am a part of you.
That's American.
Sometimes perhaps you don't want to be a part of me.
Nor do I often want to be a part of you.
But we are, that's true!
As I learn from you,
I guess you learn from me—
although you're older—and white—
and somewhat more free.

This is my page for English B.

Bessie—*Bessie Smith, a famous blues singer*
Bop—*name for a style of jazz music*
Bach—*Johann Sebastian Bach, a renown composer of classical music*

43

HARLEM

Hughes's poetry often talks about dreams, and here he speculates on the cost of not being able to pursue one's dreams. One of the phrases, "raisin in the sun," was used by playwright Lorraine Hansberry as the title of a successful play about a black family.

What happens to a dream deferred?

Does it dry up
Like a raisin in the sun?
Or fester like a sore—
And then run?
Does it stink like rotten meat?
Or crust and sugar over—
Like a syrupy sweet?

Maybe it just sags
Like a heavy load.

Or does it explode?

DRUMS

Here Hughes vividly describes two historical events, slave ships arriving in America and the birth of jazz music, and ties them in with a collective memory of African and African-American heritage.

I dream of the drums
And remember
Nights without stars in Africa.

Remember, remember, remember!

I dream of the drums
And remember
Slave ships, billowing sails,
The Western Ocean,
And the landing at Jamestown.

Remember, remember, remember!

I dream of drums
And recall, like a picture,
Congo Square in New Orleans—
Sunday—the slaves' one day of "freedom"—
The juba-dance in Congo Square.

Juba-dance—a Southern Negro dance having a lively rhythm
   and the clapping of hands

46

I dream of the drums
And hear again
Jelly Roll's piano,
Buddy Bolden's trumpet,
Kid Ory's trombone,
St. Cyr's banjo,
They join the drums…
And I remember.

Jazz!

I dream of the drums
And remember

Africa!
The ships!
New shore
And drums!

Remember!
I remember!
Remember!

Jelly Roll—*Jelly Roll Morton, a well known jazz pianist*
Buddy Bolden—*Bolden is generally considered to be the first bandleader to play improvised music, which later became known as jazz.*
Kid Ory—*a famous jazz trombone player*
St. Cyr—*Johnny St. Cyr played the banjo and guitar; he also recorded with Jelly Roll Morton.*

47

INDEX